MODELING CLAY

Bernadette Cuxart

fantasy characters

BARRON'S

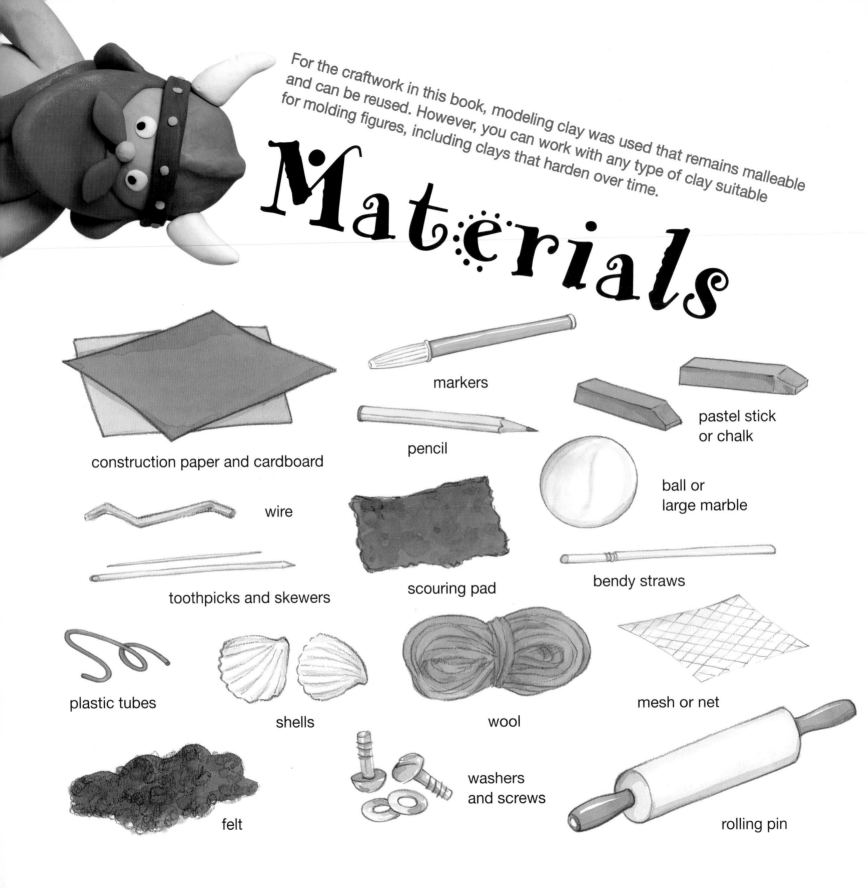

For the craftwork in this book, modeling clay was used that remains malleable and can be reused. However, you can work with any type of clay suitable for molding figures, including clays that harden over time.

Materials

construction paper and cardboard

markers

pencil

pastel stick or chalk

ball or large marble

wire

scouring pad

bendy straws

toothpicks and skewers

plastic tubes

shells

wool

mesh or net

felt

washers and screws

rolling pin

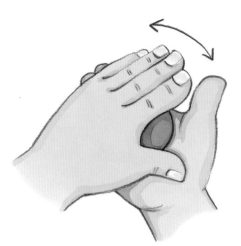

BALLS
Mold a piece of modeling clay in the palms of your hands until it forms a sphere.

SAUSAGES
If you roll a piece of modeling clay on a table with your fingers together, it will form a sausage shape. Alter the pressure you apply depending on the shape and thickness you want.

MIXING COLORS
You can create new colors by mixing modeling clay. If you mix them slightly, you will have some veined dough with which you can obtain very interesting effects. If you mix them more, you will obtain a new color.

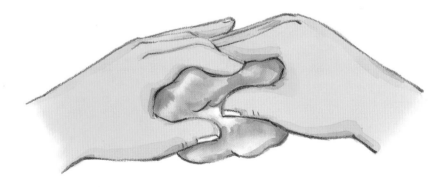

SHEETS AND TOOTHPICK SHAPES

To make flat figures, roll some modeling clay out on some plastic or paper, to prevent it from sticking to the table. Start from a ball, and flatten it with a rolling pin. To cut shapes out from a sheet, use a toothpick: First mark the shapes and then cut until they come out.

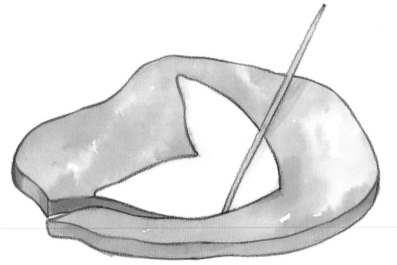

STRIPS

You can either cut the modeling clay strips from a sheet, or you can model a sausage and go over it with a rolling pin.

CUTTING

For cutting modeling clay, in addition to specific tools, you can use thread held tightly between your fingers or a piece of cardboard.

SPLASHES

To obtain a mottled effect, wet a paintbrush with runny paint and tap the brush against the handle of another paintbrush so that the paint splashes.

HAIR

To make long hair and manes, roll the wool you need around some cardboard. Tie it at one end and cut it at the other. Use a piece of wire to fix it in place.

RESISTANT JOINS

Use pieces of toothpick to join together parts that need to be strong. Then smooth the join with your fingers.

FACES

The basics of a face are simple. A little ball for the nose. A stripe made with a toothpick for the mouth (or with a skewer if you want it to be bigger). The ears are made from half a flattened ball each. And for the eyes, you have to make little balls and flatten them one over the other, smaller each time. You can add a white one at the end, to simulate a shine.

TEXTURES

Obtain a wide range of textures by pressing on the modeling clay with different materials you have at hand. For example, you can make small circles with a piece of plastic tube, and with a slightly tilted straw you can simulate scales.

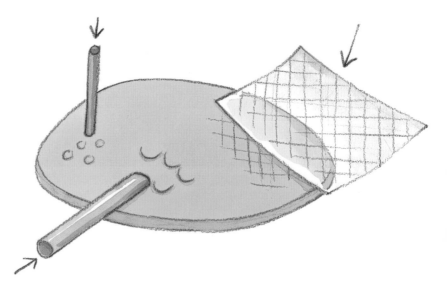

Mermaid

1. Look at the drawing and model the five parts of the mermaid's body.

2. Cut the lower part of the body diagonally and join it to the tail. Bend the tail sideways so that the mermaid is sitting down.

3. Prepare a sheet the same color as the tail and cut out the pattern on p. 35. Join this tail fin to the tail and smooth out the join. Mark the fingers with a toothpick and join the arms to the body.

1

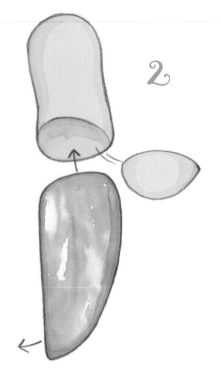

2

3

Under the sea

Mermaids live in the sea and are half fish, half woman. It is said that their song is magical... They sing very well, so much so that they can even enchant humans!

4. To make the bikini, stick on two shells. If you haven't got any, you can make it with two halves of a ball. Make the texture of the scales with a straw and mark the stripes on the tail fin with a toothpick.

4

5. Make the face (see p. 5). As the hair covers her ears, you don't need to make them. Paint some rosy cheeks on her with a pastel stick and a paintbrush.

5

6

6. Make her long hair from wool (consult p. 5). Stick it on her head with a piece of wire and join the head onto the body with a piece of toothpick. You can decorate her hair with a felt star. She will be beautiful!

Pegasus

1. Model two oval shapes and a cylinder, in the proportions shown in the drawing.

2. The cylinder is the neck, onto which you have to join the other two pieces (consult how to make joins on p. 5). To make the nose, cut the tip off the small oval and add half a white ball.

3. Make the mouth with some construction paper and the nostrils with the tip of a pencil. Fill two cardboard triangles with modeling clay for the ears. The eyes are little black balls over white ones.

4. Pierce four sausages with skewers and you have the legs. Each hoof is half a ball.

5. To make the mane, wrap some wool around some cardboard. Tie it at the top and cut it at the bottom. Stick it between the ears with a little bent wire.

6. Use the same method to make the tail. Cut out some cardboard wings using the pattern on p. 35 and stick them into its back.

Mythology

The Pegasus is a mythical animal that has enormous wings for flying. If you place a horn on its head instead, it will be a unicorn. Did you know that?

Diplodocus

1. To begin, you need a large ball and two sausages. Thin out the sausages as shown in the drawing.

2. Join the parts together as shown, using pieces of toothpick. Bend the tip of the neck to define the head.

3. Spread the modeling clay around the joins with your fingers, so that they cannot be seen. Bend the end of the tail.

4. Make the mouth with some construction paper and the eyes with the tip of a pencil.

5. Model four short sausages for the legs and stick them under the belly (consult how to make joins on p. 5). Bend the sausages a little to make the feet.

5

6

6. To finish, add some touches of chalk or pastel stick on the back, with the help of a paintbrush.

Very tall

The very long neck of the **diplodocus** enables it to eat leaves that are thirty feet above the ground. It uses its tail for support to stretch even more!

Astronaut

1. Model a square shape for the body and cut off two corners. Make a sphere for the helmet, mark a rectangle with a toothpick and hollow it out.

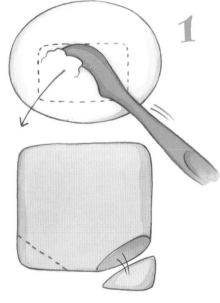

2. Mark a vertical line on the suit. Make the arms by rolling a long sausage around a short one in a spiral. Stick them onto the body (see p. 5). Strengthen the joins with a different colored sausage on each shoulder. To make the gloves, stick on some little balls and mark the thumb with a toothpick.

3. Repeat the process to make the legs. You can make the boots by joining half a ball and a cylinder together, with the help of pieces of toothpick.

Researchers

Astronauts are people from Earth who travel in rockets to discover and understand space.

4. It's time to make the face, by spreading out a little pink modeling clay. Add a little ball for the nose and make the eyes (see p. 5). Finish off the helmet with a strip of modeling clay on top and a thin sausage around the visor.

5. Simulate screws on the strip on the helmet using a skewer. Join the helmet to the body with a toothpick and add a sausage around the neck.

6. Model a cube, which will be the oxygen tank. Place it on the back and add a little ball on the cube and another on the helmet. Link two pieces of bendy straw together and stick one end in each ball.

Spaceship

1

1. Flatten clay and cut out the pattern on p. 35 using a toothpick.

2. Make the tip from another color and join the two pieces together, strengthening the join underneath. Stick on half a ball, which will be the pilot's cabin.

2

3. Surround the ball with a sausage and flatten little yellow balls on it, like a line of lights.

3

4. Place two halves of a ball on the rear part for the main lights. Mark the screws on the join with a piece of plastic tube.

4

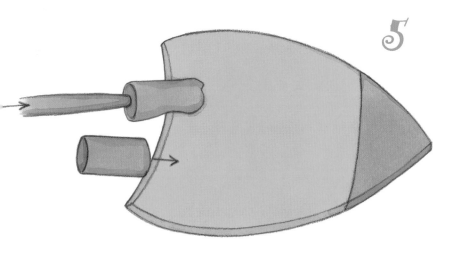

5

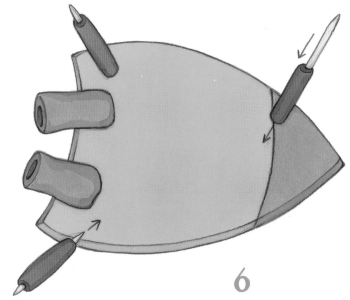

6

5. Turn the spaceship over and stick on two sausages to simulate the exhaust pipes. Strengthen the join. Make holes in the sausages with a paintbrush handle.

6. To finish, model three sausages and stick a piece of toothpick through each one. Stick one leg at the front and two at the back, slightly slanted.

With the stars

Spaceships travel the universe going through space. They go from one planet to another at great speed. Have you ever seen one? You can invent it!

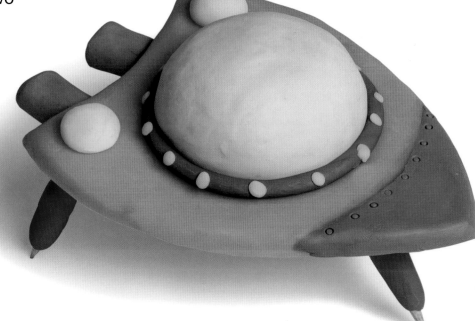

Alien

1. To begin, you need two egg-shaped pieces and three sausages. Model them looking at the drawing.

2. Stick a flattened oval onto the body to make the belly. Model the base by pressing with a pen to define the two legs.

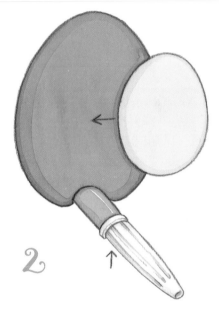

1

2

3

3. Give shape to the hands with a skewer. Stick some arms onto the body and strengthen the joins. Mark some lines on the belly with the help of a toothpick.

From beyond

You must have seen many types of aliens in books and films. Do they look like humans, or rather like animals?

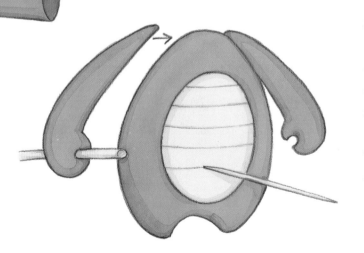

4. Stick on the tail, smooth the join, and curl the tip. To make the feet, cut a ball in half with a piece of toothpick.

5. Make the mouth with some construction paper and the nostrils with a pencil. For the eyes, place a little black sausage over a white oval. Add two sausages for the eyelids.

6. Join the head to the body with a piece of toothpick. Add the little ears at the back part and a line of plastic tubes on the top.

Troll

1

1. Model six figures in the shapes and proportions shown in the drawing.

2. Stick the legs onto the body with a piece of toothpick. Mark the toes with a skewer.

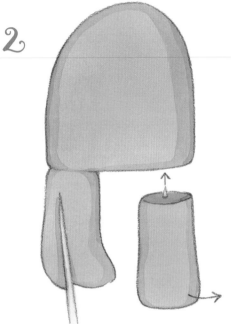

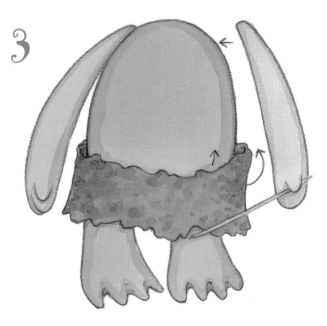

3. Cut a strip of scouring pad and roll it around the waist, pressing lightly. Stick the arms onto the body and mark the fingers with a toothpick.

4. Trolls have large red noses. Also give him a big mouth with a skewer. The eyes are flattened black balls with smaller white ones on top. Make two ears from half a ball, giving them a flat pointed shape.

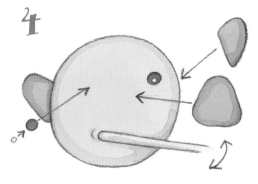

5. Make the nostril holes with a paintbrush handle. Stick a cardboard tooth in the mouth. Use wool to make the hair and the beard, and don't forget some quite broad modeling clay eyebrows.

6. Lastly, join the body to the head with a piece of skewer. Stick it slightly forward in a hunchback position.

Not very brainy

Trolls are so ugly, large, and strong that they can be scary... but in fact, they are not very clever and it is easy to distract them if they attack you.

T-Rex

1. As you can see, you need two oval shapes, a cylinder and a pointed sausage.

2. Join the neck and body and then the head and neck (consult how to make joins on p. 5).

1

2

3. Use the same technique to join the tail and the body. Now give shape to the head by flattening the nose slightly and pressing on the center with your fingers. Use a piece of construction paper to make a large open mouth.

3

4. Cut out a strip of construction paper and draw a zigzag line on it. Attach it inside the mouth for teeth. Make the nostrils with the tip of a pencil. Place two white balls for the eyes, with little black balls on top. Add two sausages for the eyelids and smooth them out.

4

5. Model two thick sausages for the back legs and stick a piece of skewer halfway through each one. Stick them onto the body and bend the bottom part backward to bend the knees. Model two triangles for the feet and mark the toes with a skewer. Join them to the legs with a piece of toothpick.

6. Model and stick on the claws. Then make two thin sausages and mark the fingers on them. Now you can stick on your T-Rex's front legs.

5

6

The most fearsome

Tyrannosaurus Rex walks only on its powerful back legs. It was a carnivore and a formidable hunter.

Extraterrestrial

1. Model six pieces in the shapes and proportions shown in the drawing. Also observe the groups of colors.

2. Join the two leg cylinders together and smooth the join at the top, so that it looks like pants. Make a belt from a different colored strip.

3. Join the two arms to the body. Make the hands by sticking half a ball onto each arm and adding some fingers made from little pieces of plastic tube.

1

Far from here

As their name suggests, extraterrestrials live far away from the Earth, on different planets. Nobody has managed to see them yet, so each of us imagines them in our own way.

2

3

4. Smooth the arm joins with your fingers. Make the feet with two triangles of modeling clay and mark the toes with a skewer. Stick them on with a piece of toothpick.

5. Make the mouth with a skewer and the nostrils with a toothpick. Flatten a white ball on the middle of the face and superimpose three more little balls. The antennae are two sausages with hollows at the top.

6. Flatten a ball on the shoulders and stick the head on with a piece of toothpick. You can apply some details to the clothing.

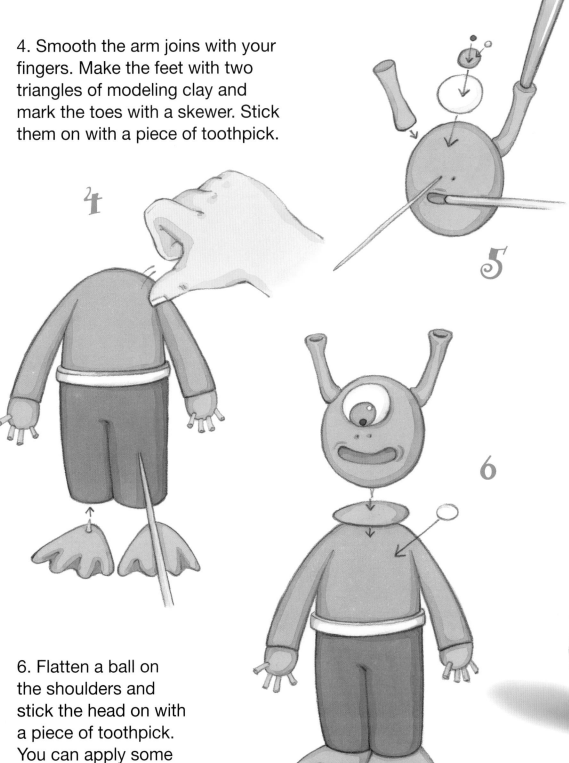

Super heroine

1. Look carefully at the shape the ten parts making the super heroine should be.
Also model them taking into account the color combination.

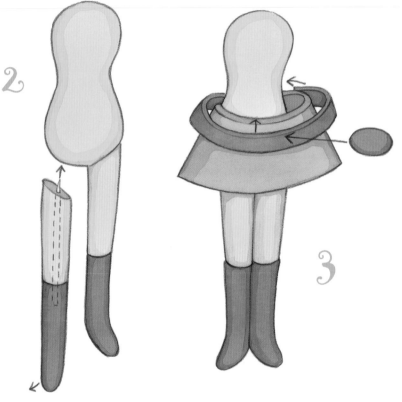

1

2

3

Who is it?

What super powers does your super heroine have? Maybe she is very strong or reads thoughts, or can fly... What is her name?

2. Pass a piece of skewer through the legs and join them to the boots. Give shape to the feet. Stick both legs onto the body and strengthen the joins well.

3. Use the pattern on p. 35 to cut out the skirt. Put it on her and join the edges at the back. Add a modeling clay belt and buckle.

4. Join two sausages together with a piece of toothpick to make each arm. Join the arms to the body and give them the shape you like. Flatten an oval to make the neckline.

5. Make the face and the hair as explained on p. 5. Also model the neck and smooth out the join with the head.

6. Stick the head onto the body with a piece of toothpick. Model some shoulder pads from two sausages. Cut out a construction paper mask using the pattern on p. 35, close it with tape, and place it on your super heroine.

Stegosaurus

1

1. Model a large ball. Make two sausages and narrow the ends, by looking at the drawing.

2. Join the parts together as shown, using pieces of toothpick (consult p. 5). Bend the tip of the neck downward to define the head.

2

3

3. Make the mouth with some construction paper, the nostrils with a toothpick, and the eyes with two little balls superimposed (black over white).

4. Model four short sausages for the legs and stick them onto the belly. Bend the sausages to simulate the feet.

4

5. Use a piece of plastic tube to mark the little circles on the skin, as if they were scales.

6. Cut out some cardboard plates in different sizes (pattern on p. 35) and stick them onto the back. To finish, add some pieces of toothpick on the tail.

5

6

With a crest

This species of dinosaur is one of the largest. The plates on its back were made of bone and the spikes on the tail served to scare off other animals, by moving its tail.

Viking

1. Model six pieces in the shapes and proportions shown in the drawing.

1

2. Join the arms to the body and mark the fingers with a toothpick. Also stick on the legs (see p. 5) and add two different colored cylinders, which will be the boots. Bend the tips to give shape to the feet.

2

3

3. Make a skirt from a thin sheet. Place a strip of modeling clay over the shoulder from front to back. Place another strip over the skirt to make a belt. Finish it off with a buckle (flattened ball).

4. Cut off part of a ball. Stick a little ball and the two parts of the moustache underneath. Make a hole under the nose with a skewer (the mouth) and superimpose two little balls for each eye. Stick on a sheet for the beard.

5. You can use the same sheet for the hair. Model the helmet from half a ball, as shown in the drawing. Add two horns on it.

6. Stick a strip of modeling clay onto the join between the helmet and the head and apply some little balls. Also make some bracelets in the same way. Join the head to the body and give it the finishing touch with a cardboard sword.

Ferocious appearance

Vikings were great sailors and brave warriors who traveled in ships shaped like dragons called "drakkars."

Dragon

1. Model four pieces in the shape and proportions shown in the drawing, all in the same color.

1

2. Join the pieces together as shown, using pieces of toothpick. Smooth out the joins until they cannot be seen.

2

3. Make the mouth with some construction paper. The eyes are made by cutting two balls and joining them together (see the drawing) and adding a little black ball at the end. Stick a modeling clay sausage on each side of the head to be the ears.

3

4. Stick on two little balls with holes in them and stick a cardboard tooth in the mouth. For the back legs, stick a ball on each side of the body. Make the front legs with toothpicks covered in modeling clay.

4

5

5. Strengthen the front legs and bend the tips slightly. Model some feet like the ones in the drawing and stick them onto the back legs. With the help of a mesh, mark the skin texture all over the body.

6

6. Cut out some cardboard triangles of different sizes and stick them along the back. On p. 35, you will find a pattern to cut some wings out of construction paper…and it's ready!

Flying dragon

You must know that dragons spit fire. Does yours, too?

Robot

1. Prepare half a ball for the head and a cylinder for the body.

2. Apply a flattened oval to the head and join it to the body. Cover the join with a sausage.

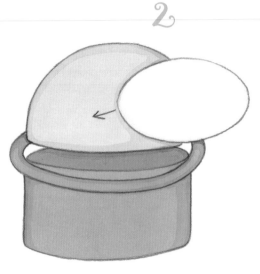

3. Model two small cylinders for the legs and half a ball for each foot. Join it all to the base of the body with toothpicks.

4. Flatten a little ball onto each side of the body and stick a piece of bendy straw into each: They are the arms. To make the hands, open two little balls with construction paper and stick them to the arms.

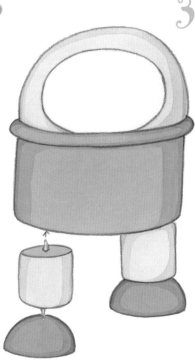

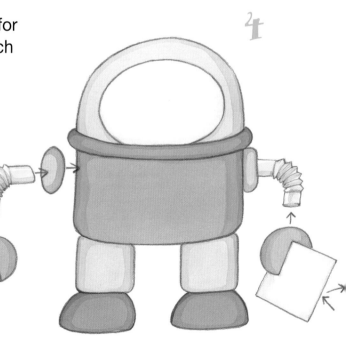

5. Use two washers for the eyes and add a little black ball to each one. Stick a screw into each side of the head. Also stick on a rectangle for the mouth.

6. Finish decorating your robot by adding another washer on the chest. You can make an antenna for him with a piece of plastic tube stuck on with a little modeling clay ball.

Good helpers

Robots are machines programmed to carry out certain tasks. Some are very intelligent. They can do many things and they save us a lot of work.

Dinosaur eggs

1. To make an open egg, wrap a ball in a plastic bag and cover it halfway with modeling clay. Remove it to make the open half of the eggshell.

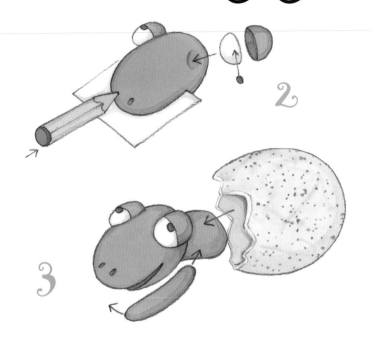

2. Model an oval shape for the dinosaur's head. Make the mouth with some construction paper and the nostrils with a pencil. Model a colored ball and another white one, cut them in half and join the different halves together. Add a little black ball to each eye and stick them on the head, in some small hollows.

3. Stick on a piece of body and two legs. Paint the egg (see p. 4) and place the dinosaur inside, as if it had just hatched.

Patterns

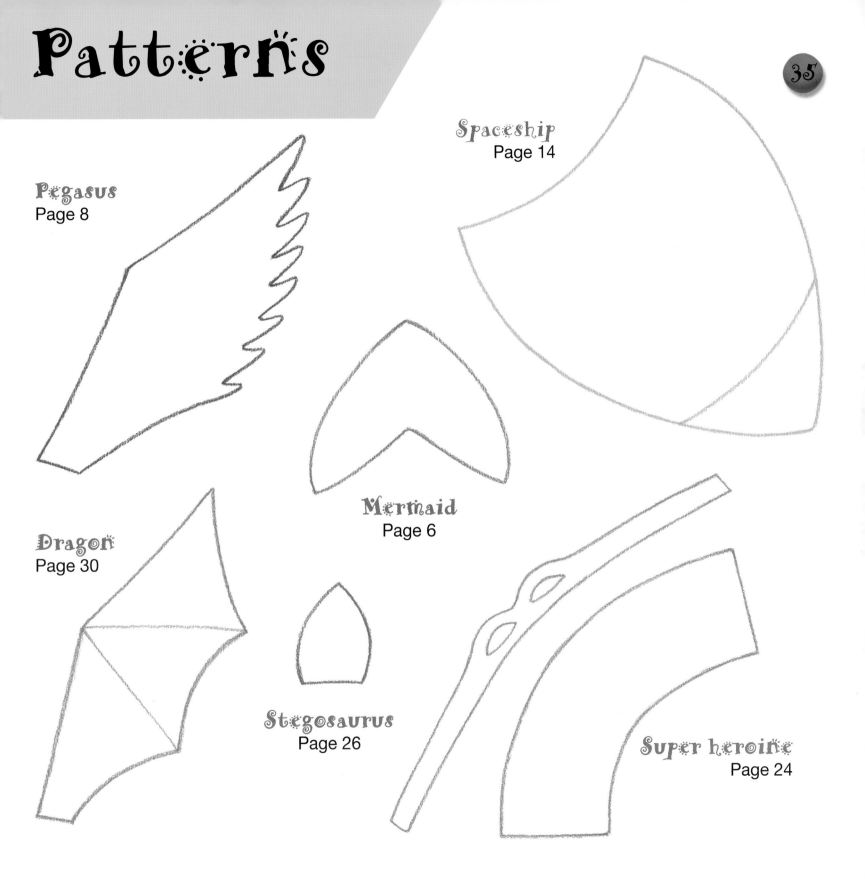

Pegasus
Page 8

Spaceship
Page 14

Mermaid
Page 6

Dragon
Page 30

Stegosaurus
Page 26

Super heroine
Page 24

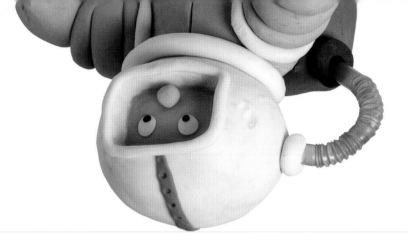

First edition for the United States and Canada published in 2013 by Barron's Educational Series, Inc.

Original title of the book in Catalan: *Modela Personatges de Fantasia*
© Copyright GEMSER PUBLICATIONS S.L., 2013
C/ Castell, 38; Teià (08329) Barcelona, Spain
   (World Rights)
Tel: 93 540 13 53
E-mail: info@mercedesros.com
Website: www.mercedesros.com

Author and Illustrator: Bernadette Cuxart

All inquiries should be addressed to:
Barron's Educational Series, Inc.
250 Wireless Boulevard
Hauppauge, New York 11788
www.barronseduc.com

ISBN: 978-1-4380-0357-3

Library of Congress Control Number: 2013934484

Date of Manufacture: May 2013
Manufactured by: L. REX PRINTING COMPANY
   LIMITED, Dongguan City, Guangdong, China

Printed in China
9 8 7 6 5 4 3 2 1